little bigfoot

an imprint of sasquatch books
seattle, wa

Design and Illustration by Moxey Creative Ltd

Printed in Colombia

LITTLE BIGFOOT with colophon is a registered trademark of Blue Star Press, LLC

30 29 28 27 26   9 8 7 6 5 4 3 2 1

The authorized representative in the EU for product safety and compliance is Authorised Rep Compliance Ltd., Ground Floor, 71 Lower Baggot Street, Dublin D02 P593, Ireland. www.arccompliance.com

A catalog record for this book is available from the Library of Congress upon request.

ISBN: 978-1-63217-634-9

Design by Sarah Baynes
Text by L.J. Tracosas
Photo research by Micah Schmidt
Copyediting by Laura Whittemore
Proofreading by Jen Swanson

Sasquatch Books
1325 Fourth Avenue, Suite 1025
Seattle, WA 98101

SasquatchBooks.com

Please note that statistics can vary between sources and may not always be comprehensively recorded, especially for earlier seasons or certain competitions. The figures within this book are based on available data and will be subject to updates as more information becomes available.

CONTENTS

HOW WILL YOU CHOOSE YOUR
G.O.A.T.?

BOOM! The crowd erupts as the ball hits the back of the net. **WHOOSH!** A defender makes a sliding tackle that stops a sure goal. **INCREDIBLE!** A goalkeeper stretches to make a fingertip save that defies gravity.

Welcome to the electrifying world of soccer superstars—the players who make us jump out of our seats, hold our breath, and debate for hours about who truly deserves the title of **G.O.A.T. (Greatest of All Time)!**

This book takes you on a thrilling journey through the lives and careers of today's most jaw-dropping soccer talents. You'll discover their childhood struggles, witness their breakthrough moments, and celebrate their greatest triumphs. By the final page, you'll have all the ammunition you need to defend YOUR choice of the **ultimate soccer superstar**.

But here's the thing—**there's no "correct answer"** when picking your G.O.A.T. While some fans might obsess over goal tallies and trophy cabinets, others might be drawn to a player's incredible life story. Maybe you'll choose someone who represents your home country, or perhaps you'll be captivated by a player who overcame impossible obstacles to reach the top.

Some fans value what players do off the field—their charity work, how they treat their fans, or how they stand up for important causes. Others might be impressed by a player's loyalty to one club or how they inspire their teammates. And yes, some of us just can't resist that player who scores spectacular goals that seem to defy physics!

Soccer stardom comes in all shapes and sizes. While forwards often steal the headlines with their goal-scoring heroics, midfielders are the engine room of any team—controlling the tempo, threading needle-perfect passes, and adding their own scoring punch. Defenders turn attack into defense with bone-crunching tackles and split-second decision-making, while goalkeepers can single-handedly save the day with lightning-fast reflexes and fearless diving saves.

Don't forget to check out our **"Top Talent"** lists at the back of this book. You'll find incredible players from every position—including those unsung heroes who might not grab the spotlight but are essential to their team's success. After all, even the brightest superstars need teammates to pass to, and it's the TEAM that lifts the trophy when the final whistle blows!

Now, let's dive into the lives of these soccer legends and discover what makes them so extraordinary. Who knows? Your G.O.A.T. might be waiting on the very next page.

LAMINE YAMAL

Born in Catalonia, Spain, Lamine Yamal Nasraoui Ebana's name honors two people who supported his family before his birth. When he scores, watch for his special "304" celebration—a tribute to his childhood zip code and the community that raised him.

At just seven years old, Yamal left home to train at Barcelona's legendary La Masia academy. While most kids were mastering hopscotch, he was competing against teenagers! These challenging matchups forged his **extraordinary skills**, transforming him from a goal-scoring youngster into a dribbling wizard with a gift for setting up teammates.

At 15, Yamal became the youngest player in 100 years to debut for Barcelona's first team. Then, at sixteen, he made history again as the **youngest player ever nominated for the prestigious Golden Boy award**. Yamal often had to prioritise homework over football. Can you imagine? "Sorry, can't accept this world-famous award tonight . . . math problems due tomorrow!"

2024 brought even more milestones as Yamal became the **youngest player ever to play in a European Championship** AND the youngest to score in one! To top it all off, he finally claimed that Golden Boy award (hopefully after finishing his assignments).

With lightning-fast footwork and vision beyond his years, Yamal isn't just playing soccer—**he's rewriting the record books** before he's even old enough to drive. One thing's certain: this is just the beginning of an incredible journey for Spain's young superstar!

Lamine Yamal is already known for his **awesome dribbling skills**, using fancy footwork to get past defenders and score amazing goals. Barcelona knows exactly what they have in this teenage phenom. They're so sure he's the real deal that they slapped a **BILLION-DOLLAR** release clause in his contract! That's right—any club wanting to steal Yamal away would need to cough up more than $1,000,000,000! Talk about a vote of confidence from one of the world's greatest clubs.

Club Team:
FC Barcelona (Spain)

International Team:
Spain

19

Club Shirt Number

Previous Clubs
⚽ Barcelona B (Spain)

Player Award Highlights
⚽ Golden Boy (2024)
⚽ La Liga U23 Player of the Season (2023-24)
⚽ The Best FIFA Men's 11 (2024)

Team Award Highlights
⚽ La Liga (2022-23)
⚽ UEFA European Championship (2024)
⚽ Supercopa de España (2025)

Career Stats
⚽ Career Appearances: 134
⚽ Career Goals: 29
⚽ Career Assists: 43

LAMINE YAMAL

POSITION:
ATTACKING MIDFIELDER

FUN FACT:
At the age of 16, Yamal was the youngest player to win a major international trophy (Euros 2024).

KYLIAN MBAPPÉ

Born in the heart of Paris, Kylian Mbappé exploded onto the soccer scene as a teenager. First playing for AS Monaco, he helped them win the Ligue 1 title in the 2016-17 season. At 18, he signed for Paris Saint-Germain (PSG) in a deal worth nearly 200 million dollars, making him the most expensive teenager ever at the time!

His time at PSG was nothing short of legendary. **He racked up more than 200 goals**, becoming the club's all-time leading scorer and helping them dominate French soccer. In the 2019-20 season, his brilliance led PSG to a domestic quadruple—four major trophies in a single year!

While conquering club soccer, Mbappé also **led France to World Cup glory in 2018**, and his amazing performances earned him the FIFA World Cup Best Young Player and French Player of the Year awards.

When he finally made his dream move to Real Madrid, **the pressure was immense**. Every touch was scrutinized, every miss magnified. But champions rise to challenges! Instead of crumbling, Mbappé worked tirelessly to adapt to his new team.

By early 2025, **the soccer world witnessed the return of his unstoppable form**— a powerful reminder that true greatness isn't about avoiding pressure, but thriving under it!

Kylian Mbappé is famous for his **explosive pace** and his ability to turn his runs into goals, speeding past defenders before they even have a chance to react. He's also a **natural leader** in the locker room, becoming **France's captain**, and he always steps up for his team when it matters the most.

Club Team:
Real Madrid (Spain)

International Team:
France (Captain)

9

Club Shirt Number

Previous Clubs

⚽ AS Monaco (Monaco)
⚽ Paris Saint-Germain (France)

Player Award Highlights

⚽ FIFA World Cup Golden Boot (2022)
⚽ 4 x French Player of the Year (2018, '19, '22-23, '23-24)
⚽ FIFA World Cup Silver Ball (2022)

Team Award Highlights

⚽ FIFA World Cup (2018)
⚽ FIFA Intercontinental Cup (2024)
⚽ UEFA Nations League (2020-21)

Career Stats

⚽ Career Appearances: 525
⚽ Career Goals: 381
⚽ Career Assists: 165

KYLIAN MBAPPÉ

POSITION:
FORWARD

FUN FACT:
Mbappé is a good friends with
NBA star LeBron James!

They call him "The Flea"—not because he's tiny (though at 5'7" he's not the tallest), but because he's IMPOSSIBLE to catch! Born in Rosario, Argentina, Lionel Messi started dazzling with a soccer ball at just four years old!

Growing up, Messi faced a serious challenge—a growth hormone deficiency that meant his body wasn't developing like those of other kids his age. But this setback became part of his **legendary story**. At 13, his supernatural talent caught FC Barcelona's eye, and they didn't just invite him to join their famous academy—they even helped pay for his medical treatments!

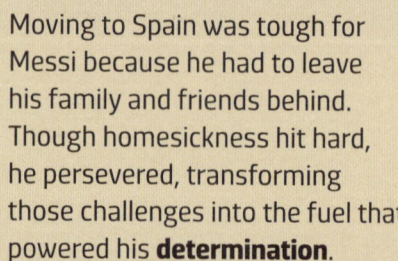

Moving to Spain was tough for Messi because he had to leave his family and friends behind. Though homesickness hit hard, he persevered, transforming those challenges into the fuel that powered his **determination**.

What followed was nothing short of **EXTRAORDINARY**! At Barcelona, Messi became the cornerstone of possibly the greatest club team ever assembled, collecting trophies like other kids collect trading cards. His low center of gravity, combined with lightning-quick feet and mind-blowing ball control, made him practically unstoppable.

After legendary runs with Barcelona and Paris Saint-Germain, Messi took his talents to the USA for Inter Miami CF. But his greatest soccer moment? **Leading Argentina to World Cup glory in 2022**—the one trophy that had eluded him for so long!

Many people consider Messi one of the greatest soccer players of all time. From a small boy with big dreams and medical challenges to one of the most celebrated athletes in history, Messi's journey proves that **with enough heart, skill, and determination, anything is possible**.

Lionel Messi has had an amazing career, leading his country, Argentina, to the **ultimate achievement** in soccer by winning the World Cup in 2022. With **more than 850 goals**, he's one of the highest goal scorers of all time. His incredible achievements have been recognized, and **he's won the Ballon d'Or a record eight times**.

Club Team:
Inter Miami CF (USA)

International Team:
Argentina

10

Club Shirt Number

Previous Clubs

- ⚽ Paris Saint-Germaine (France)
- ⚽ FC Barcelona (Spain)
- ⚽ Newell's Old Boys (Argentina)

Player Award Highlights

- ⚽ 1 x FIFA World Player of the Year
- ⚽ 2 x FIFA World Cup Golden Ball (2014, '22)
- ⚽ 8 x Ballon D'ors (2009, '10, '11, '12, '15, '19, '21, '23)

Team Award Highlights

- ⚽ 10 x La Liga (FC Barcelona)
- ⚽ 4 x UEFA Champions League (FC Barcelona)
- ⚽ 1 x Leagues Cup (Inter Miami)
- ⚽ 1 x Olympic Gold Medal (Argentina)
- ⚽ 1 x FIFA World Cup (Argentina)

Career Stats

- ⚽ Career Appearances: 1,125
- ⚽ Career Goals: 871
- ⚽ Career Assists: 424

LIONEL MESSI

POSITION:
FORWARD

FUN FACT:
Messi's first contract for Barcelona was written in a restaurant, on a napkin. The napkin later sold at auction for $965,000.

Born on the island of Madeira, Portugal, Cristiano Ronaldo kicked off his soccer journey at the local club where his father worked. Even as a boy, his extraordinary talent was obvious—though few could have predicted the incredible heights he would reach!

As a teenager, Ronaldo faced a terrifying challenge when doctors discovered a racing **heart condition** that threatened to end his career before it truly began. After undergoing heart surgery, he bounced back stronger than ever—a sign of the **unstoppable determination** that would define his career.

After **impressing** at Sporting Lisbon, where he jumped between several youth teams before joining the first team in 2002, his talent quickly caught the eye of many clubs.

He ultimately signed with Manchester United in England, where he transformed from a flashy teenager into a **goal-scoring machine**, netting an incredible 42 goals in the 2007-08 season and winning both the Golden Shoe and FIFA World Player of the Year!

He went on to win the 2008 FIFA Club World Cup with Manchester United. And in 2024, Ronaldo scored his 900th career goal, making him the **first men's player to reach such a lofty achievement**.

Ronaldo's international career with Portugal spans an astonishing 20+ years, highlighted by captaining his country to European Championship glory in 2016. He became the **first player EVER to score in five different World Cups**—just one of countless records this unstoppable legend has set throughout his remarkable career!

Cristiano Ronaldo has scored more than **900 goals** and won countless awards throughout his career, but those who have worked with him often say his biggest strength is his **mental focus and attitude**. This mindset has helped him to keep pushing forward throughout his career.

Club Team:
Al-Nassr (Saudi Arabia)

International Team:
Portugal

7

Club Shirt Number

Previous Clubs

- ⚽ Sporting CP (Portugal)
- ⚽ Manchester United (England)
- ⚽ Real Madrid (Spain)
- ⚽ Juventus (Italy)

Player Award Highlights

- ⚽ Golden Foot (2020)
- ⚽ Premier League Golden Boot (2007-08)
- ⚽ FIFA Club World Cup Golden Ball (2016)

Team Award Highlights

- ⚽ 3 x Premier League Titles (2006-07, '07-'08, '08-'09)
- ⚽ 1 x UEFA European Championship (2016)
- ⚽ 5 x UEFA Champions League (2007-08, '13-'14, '15-'16, '16-'17, '17-'18)

Career Stats

- ⚽ Career Appearances: 1,273
- ⚽ Career Goals: 931
- ⚽ Career Assists: 288

CRISTIANO RONALDO

POSITION:
FORWARD

FUN FACT:
Ronaldo's father named him after the former U.S. President Ronald Reagan.

Born in Stourbridge, England, Jude Bellingham wasn't instantly obsessed with soccer like some superstar players. But once he caught the bug, he really took to it. He joined Birmingham City FC as a young child, where he rose through the youth ranks.

At just 17, Bellingham turned down an offer to play for Manchester United to join **Borussia Dortmund**, choosing to focus on bigger challenges rather than a bigger paycheck. Although he was still well-paid at Dortmund!

In Bellingham's very first game with Dortmund, he became the club's youngest-ever goalscorer at that time. His **midfield dominance** continued to grow, and by the 2022-23 season, he swept up both the prestigious **Golden Boy and Kopa Trophy awards**—recognizing him as the best young player in world soccer!

After making steady progress with Dortmund, Bellingham made the massive leap to Spanish giants **Real Madrid** in 2023, signing a six-year deal that promised to take his career to new heights.

He made an instant impact, becoming the club's lead goalscorer in his first year and **helping them win both the Champions League and La Liga title that season**. His stats show he can dominate even at a young age, playing with the best and reaching the finals of the UEFA European Championship in both 2020 and 2024, with England.

Jude Bellingham is a **complete midfielder**, known for his precise passing and ability to make **crucial sliding interceptions** right under his opponent's feet. His career has been a steady climb, and in his early 20s, he shows no signs of slowing down.

Club Team:
Real Madrid (Spain)

International Team:
England

5

Club Shirt Number

Previous Clubs

⚽ Birmingham City FC (England)
⚽ Borussia Dortmund (Germany)

Player Award Highlights

⚽ Golden Boy (2023)
⚽ La Liga Player of the Season (2023-24)
⚽ The Best FIFA Men's 11 (2024)

Team Award Highlights

⚽ UEFA Champions League (2023-24)
⚽ FIFA Intercontinental Cup (2024)
⚽ La Liga (2023-24)

Career Stats

⚽ Career Appearances: 313
⚽ Career Goals: 71
⚽ Career Assists: 64

JUDE BELLINGHAM

POSITION:
MIDFIELDER

FUN FACT:
Jude's younger brother Jobe is also a professional soccer player and is signed with Sunderland AFC, in the English Football League.

AITANA BONMATÍ

Born in Spain with a fighting spirit in her DNA, Aitana Bonmatí made history before she even kicked a ball! Her parents battled traditional naming customs to put her mother's surname first—a revolutionary act that foreshadowed Aitana's boundary-breaking career.

Unlike other kids who played soccer for fun, young Bonmatí was **a perfectionist to her core**, and she demanded excellence from herself in every practice, every drill, every match. When other children shrugged off mistakes, Bonmatí analyzed what went wrong and worked obsessively to fix it.

When she joined CD Ribes and discovered they had no girls' team, she jumped straight into matches with just boys—holding her own and **proving her skills** belonged on any field with ANY competition.

Bonmatí is passionate about taking care of both her mind and body. Her parents encouraged a balanced development—sharpening her mind through reading and learning, while honing her soccer skills. Her discipline off the field has translated into discipline on the field, making her a key asset to her team.

With her talent and determination, Barcelona Femení (FC Barcelona's women's team) has achieved incredible success, including three trebles, a continental quadruple, and the team's first Champions League title in 2021, where Bonmatí was named **MVP** (Most Valuable Player) of the final.

Aitana Bonmatí has played for both Catalonia and Spain. She's a super versatile player who can adapt to whatever her team needs. She won the **Ballon d'Or Féminin** and **Best FIFA Women's Player** in both 2023 and 2024. In the 2023-24 season, she became the **most-decorated female soccer player in a single season**, ever!

Club Team:
FC Barcelona (Spain)

International Team:
Spain

14

Club Shirt Number

Previous Clubs

⚽ CD Ribes (Spain)

Player Award Highlights

⚽ The Best FIFA Women's Player (2023, '24)
⚽ FIFA Women's World Cup Golden Ball (2023)
⚽ The Best FIFA Women's 11 (2024)
⚽ UEFA Women's Player of the Year (2022-23)

Team Award Highlights

⚽ Supercopa de España (2019-20, '21-'22, '22-'23, '23-'24)
⚽ FIFA Women's World Cup (2023)
⚽ UEFA Women's Champions League (2020-21, '22-'23, '23-'24)
⚽ UEFA Women's Nations League (2023-24)

Career Stats

⚽ Career Appearances: 317
⚽ Career Goals: 112
⚽ Career Assists: 87

AITANA BONMATÍ

POSITION:
MIDFIELDER

FUN FACT:
At the age of seven, Bonmatí joined her local team, CD Ribes. There were more than 400 boys in the academy, and she was the only girl.

MOHAMED SALAH

Born in Egypt with soccer dreams bigger than the pyramids, Mohamed Salah's journey to superstardom required extraordinary dedication. As a kid, his passion for the game was so intense that he'd travel for hours every day just to train with Arab Contractors.

His sacrifice paid off at 17 when he made history as the **youngest-ever player** to debut in the Egyptian Premier League with Al Mokawloon Al Arab.

After representing Egypt in the Olympics in 2012, Salah took his talents to Europe, beginning in Switzerland with club Basel. There, he quickly made his mark, helping the team capture **two league titles** and catching the eyes of bigger clubs.

Next, Salah transferred to **Chelsea FC** in England, but the move turned into a frustrating experience with limited playing time and a manager who didn't appreciate his talents and left Salah warming the bench. So, **he reinvented himself** in Italy with Fiorentina, where he chose jersey number 74 to honor the victims of a tragic event in Cairo.

He then played for Roma before making his way back to England with Liverpool FC. Since joining Liverpool, Salah has found his form, winning the **trophies** and **titles** he always dreamed of.

Mohamed Salah has the perfect mix of **speed and power**, and his goals have played a big part in helping Liverpool win many trophies. Along the way, he's picked up the **Golden Ball**, **Golden Foot**, and **three Premier League Golden Boots**. It took him years and several teams, but Salah has proven his commitment to the game, no matter where he's playing.

Club Team:
Liverpool (England)

International Team:
Egypt

11

Club Shirt Number

Previous Clubs

- Al-Mokawloon (Egypt)
- Basel (Switzerland)
- Chelsea (England)
- Fiorentina (Italy)
- Roma (Italy)

Player Award Highlights

- Golden Foot (2021)
- FIFA Club World Cup Golden Ball (2019)
- Time 100 (2019)
- Premier League Golden Boot (2017-18, '18-'19*, '21-'22*) *shared*

Team Award Highlights

- FIFA Club World Cup (2019)
- UEFA Champions League (2018-19)
- Premier League (2019-20)

Career Stats

- Career Appearances: 756
- Career Goals: 380
- Career Assists: 195

MOHAMED SALAH

POSITION:
FORWARD

FUN FACT:
In 2018, The British Museum displayed a pair of Salah's soccer boots alongside their Ancient Egypt collection.

Sam Kerr launched her pro career at age 15 with Perth Glory FC. After a brief stint with Sydney WC, her extraordinary talent took her across the ocean to the Western New York Flash in the United States—but Australia's golden girl eventually returned home to Perth.

Back on familiar turf, Kerr's game exploded to new heights. Her skills were sharper than ever, racking up **tons of goals and awards**. She later played in the U.S. continuing her scoring streak.

With a reputation as **one of the world's most lethal finishers**, it was only a matter of time before European powerhouse Chelsea FC came calling.

At Chelsea, Kerr's brilliance helped power the Blues to the 2019-20 League title, followed by an incredible **three consecutive Women's Super League championships**!

On the international stage, Kerr made history in 2019 by becoming **the first Australian to score a hat-trick in a World Cup tournament**. As Australia's captain, she led the team to a historic fourth place finish at the 2020 Olympic Games, their best performance at the time.

Sam Kerr has become a powerhouse striker, amazing fans with her signature **backlfip celebration** every time she scores. She has dominated on the field both in club soccer and has been made **captain** of her national team, **Australia**.

Club Team:
Chelsea FC (England)

International Team:
Australia (Captain)

20

Club Shirt Number

Previous Clubs

- ⚽ Perth Glory FC (Australia)
- ⚽ Western NY Flash (USA)
- ⚽ Sky Blue FC (USA)
- ⚽ Chicago Red Stars (USA)

Player Award Highlights

- ⚽ W-League Golden Boot (2017-18, '18-'19)
- ⚽ NWSL Golden Boot (2017, '18, '19)
- ⚽ FIFA FIFPRO Women's World 11 (2022, '23)

Team Award Highlights

- ⚽ FA Women's Super League (2019-20, '20-'21, '21-'22, '22-'23, '23-'24)
- ⚽ Women's FA Cup (2020-21, '21-'22, '22-'23)
- ⚽ FA Women's League Cup (2019-20, '20-'21)

Career Stats

- ⚽ Career Appearances: 314
- ⚽ Career Goals: 250
- ⚽ Career Assists: 20

SAM KERR

POSITION:
FORWARD

FUN FACT:
In 2023, Kerr made history as the first female
soccer player to appear on the global
cover of the FIFA console game series.

RODRI

Born near Madrid as Rodrigo Hernández Cascante, Rodri's soccer journey began early at age 11 with youth powerhouse Atlético Madrid. By his teens, scouts worried about one major problem—was he physically strong enough to compete at the highest level?

After being let go from Atlético Madrid, Rodri began playing for Villarreal, he hit a growth spurt that transformed him from questionable prospect to can't-miss star. Atlético Madrid quickly realized their mistake and brought him back for a year before Manchester City FC paid to secure him on a long-term deal. His impact was so strong that his manager declared him **"irreplaceable"**—possibly the highest compliment in professional sports!

Even as his soccer career took off, Rodri took his education seriously. Though soccer is his passion, he believes that **there's more to life than just football.** This is a thoughtful perspective that gives him a unique vision on the field.

While he's not a flashy goal-scorer, Rodri's brilliance lies in his intelligence, positioning, and **ability to control the game's tempo**. His support play and assists create countless opportunities for teammates, while his defensive work frequently breaks up opposing attacks before they become dangerous.

He won the Ballon d'Or in 2024 for his efforts, reminding the soccer world that sometimes the most valuable player isn't the one scoring the most goals, but the one making everyone around them better.

Rodri isn't afraid to get physical with his defensive style. He wins tackles all over the pitch, acting as a **solid backbone** for his team from his midfield position. His ability to play **strong defense** while also being effective going forward makes him **one of the best midfielders in the world**.

Club Team:
Manchester City FC
(England)

International Team:
Spain

16

Club Shirt Number

Previous Clubs
- ⚽ Villareal CF (Spain)
- ⚽ Atlético Madrid (Spain)

Player Award Highlights
- ⚽ Ballon d'Or Winner (2024)
- ⚽ The Best FIFA Men's 11 (2024)
- ⚽ FIFA Club World Cup Golden Ball (2023)
- ⚽ Globe Soccer Awards Best Midfielder of the Year (2023)

Team Award Highlights
- ⚽ FIFA Club World Cup (2023)
- ⚽ Premier League (2020-21, '21-'22, '22-'23, '23-'24)
- ⚽ UEFA Champions League (2022-23)

Career Stats
- ⚽ Career Appearances: 491
- ⚽ Career Goals: 37
- ⚽ Career Assists: 40

RODRI

POSITION:
MIDFIELDER

FUN FACT:
Rodri's brilliant goal in the 2023 Champions League final clinched Manchester City's first-ever UCL title.

SALMA PARALLUELO

Born in Zaragoza, Spain, Salma Paralluelo isn't just a talented soccer player—she's a two-sport superstar! She won two gold medals as a sprinter at the 2019 European Youth Summer Olympic Festival.

While training for athletics competitions, Paralluelo simultaneously made waves in soccer, starting with hometown club Zaragoza CF before moving to **Villareal CF** to face tougher competition.

In 2022, she made the **career-defining decision** to sign with powerhouse FC Barcelona, fully committing to soccer.

At Barcelona, Paralluelo helped the team win the UEFA Champions League twice (2022-23 and 2023-24), along with several other major trophies. Her international career has been even more historic: she played pivotal roles in Spain's victories at the FIFA U17 Women's World Cup (2018), the FIFA U20 Women's World Cup (2022), and the 2023 FIFA Women's World Cup, becoming **the first player ever to win all three versions of the World Cup**.

Her track background clearly gave her an edge on the soccer field— **explosive sprint speed** that leaves defenders in the dust. Now fully focused on soccer, Paralluelo's combination of athletic gifts and soccer skills makes her one of the **most exciting young talents** in the world game!

Salma Paralluelo has become an expert at handling one-on-ones, delivering and receiving goal-scoring passes, and finding space to score. As a **FIFA Women's World Cup winner** in 2023, she's still young and definitely **a player to watch** in the years to come.

Club Team:
FC Barcelona (Spain)

International Team:
Spain

7

Club Shirt Number

Previous Clubs

- Zaragoza CF (Spain)
- Villareal CF (Spain)

Player Award Highlights

- The Best FIFA Women's 11 (2024)
- FIFA Women's World Cup Young Player Award (2023)
- U18 400 Meter Indoor Track

Team Award Highlights

- UEFA Women's Champions League (2022-23, '23-'24)
- FIFA Women's World Cup (2023)
- Supercopa de España (2022-23, '23-'24)

Career Stats

- Career Appearances: 96
- Career Goals: 62
- Career Assists: 10

SALMA PARALLUELO

POSITION:
FORWARD

FUN FACT:
Paralluelo's background as a sprinter makes her one of the fastest players in women's soccer, often leaving defenders in the dust.

VINÍCIUS JÚNIOR

Born in São Gonçalo, a city in Rio de Janeiro, Brazil, Vinícius Júnior's journey began with big dreams but limited resources. But at just 10 years old, he joined the famous Flamengo academy, where his journey in soccer began.

By 16, Vinícius Júnior was **dazzling scouts** at the junior Copa São Paulo and dominating the South American U17 Championship, where he was crowned **Best Player** of the tournament.

His **electrifying performances** caught the attention of Real Madrid, who signed him at age 16, though they had to wait a couple of years for him to join the team due to age restrictions.

When he finally arrived in Madrid, Vinícius faced enormous pressure—he was expected to fill the shoes of Cristiano Ronaldo on the left wing. His early years were tough, as he struggled to adapt to the elite level. **Fans grew frustrated**, teammates hesitated to pass to him, and doubters questioned if he was **worth the hype**.

But instead of crumbling, Vinícius showed incredible **mental strength**. After spending time out of the starting lineup, he redoubled his efforts in training, determined to prove everyone wrong.

His breakthrough came in the 2021-22 season, when his performances skyrocketed to new heights. The crowning moment? **Scoring the winning goal** in the UEFA Champions League final against Liverpool—transforming from questioned prospect to certified Madrid hero in one magical moment.

Vinícius Júnior once found himself caught up in drama with his teammates and the club's fans. Instead of letting it bring him down, **he used the negative comments as motivation**. He took the criticism and turned it into fuel, pushing himself to improve and **exceed expectations**.

Club Team:
Real Madrid (Spain)

International Team:
Brazil

7

Club Shirt Number

Previous Clubs

⚽ Flamengo (Brazil)

Player Award Highlights

⚽ FIFA Club World Cup Golden Ball (2022)
⚽ The Best FIFA Men's Player (2024)
⚽ FIFA Intercontinental Cup Golden Ball (2024)

Team Award Highlights

⚽ FIFA Club World Cup (2018, '22)
⚽ UEFA Champions League (2021-22, '23-'24)
⚽ La Liga (2019-20, '21-'22, '23-'24)

Career Stats

⚽ Career Appearances: 429
⚽ Career Goals: 129
⚽ Career Assists: 93

VINÍCIUS JÚNIOR

POSITION:
FORWARD

FUN FACT:
Vinícius scored the match-winning goal
in the 2022 UEFA Champions League final,
helping to win Real Madrid's 14th title.

Born in South Korea, Son Heung-min's path to stardom was anything but conventional! While most future stars were playing in matches and tournaments from a young age, Son wasn't even allowed to play in soccer matches until he was a teenager!

His father, who became his first coach, believed in a completely different training philosophy. Instead of game experience, Son spent years perfecting his **technical skills**, focusing purely on ball handling.

At 16, he left FC Seoul and moved across the world to Germany to join Hamburger SV. After a brief return to South Korea to play in the **FIFA U17 World Cup**, he headed back to Germany where his unique technical foundation began to shine, and Bayer Leverkusen signed him.

Son continued to impress, even **scoring a hat trick** against his former club, Hamburger SV.

In his early 20s, **Tottenham Hotspur** spotted him and brought him to the Premier League in England. His dazzling performances culminated in winning the Premier League **Golden Boot** in 2022 with 23 goals and making history as the first Asian player to score 100 Premier League goals!

Son Heung-min has proven himself as a force on the field with his **incredible ball control**, even at high speeds. His ability to beat multiple defenders and score impressive goals has made him a **standout player**. As the captain of South Korea's national team, he's become **a symbol of pride** for his country.

Club Team:
Tottenham Hotspur
(captain, England)

International Team:
South Korea (captain)

7

Club Shirt Number

Previous Clubs

- FC Seoul (South Korea)
- Hamburger SV (Germany)

Player Award Highlights

- Premier League Golden Boot (2021-22)
- Best Footballer in Asia (2014, '15, '17, '18, '19, '20, '21, '22, '23)
- AFC Asian International Player of the Year (2015, '17, '19, '23)

Team Award Highlights

- Asian Games (2018)
- UEFA Champions League runner-up (2018-19)
- EFL Cup runner-up (2020-21)

Career Stats

- Career Appearances: 785
- Career Goals: 289
- Career Assists: 138

SON HEUNG-MIN

POSITION:
FORWARD

FUN FACT:
In 2020, Son completed South Korea's compulsory military training, coming top of his class in shooting and endurance exercises.

Growing up in Brazil, young Neymar honed his skills by playing futsal, a lightning-fast version of soccer played on a hard court with a smaller, heavier ball. In these tight spaces, players have split seconds to react, teaching Neymar the quick thinking and near-magical ball control he developed.

Born into a family that struggled financially, Neymar's extraordinary talent transformed his family's lives, too. Still a teenager playing for Santos FC, he **helped them afford their first real home**.

At just 17, Neymar made his professional debut and quickly gained attention with his flair for the game. Even as European giants like Chelsea came calling with big-money offers, Neymar made the **mature decision** to continue developing in Brazil before making the leap overseas.

When he finally joined FC Barcelona at 21, he made an **immediate impact**. In the 2014-15 season, Neymar played alongside legends Lionel Messi and Luis Suárez, helping his team win a domestic treble, including two trophies and a league title.

In 2017, Neymar moved to Paris Saint-Germain (PSG) for a fresh challenge. Despite battling injuries throughout his career, Neymar set a record in 2024 for the **most goals scored by any player for Brazil's national team**, an achievement that places him among the true legends of the beautiful game.

Neymar is famous for his incredible skills and tricks, using his body to create opportunities for himself and his teammates. Want to learn one of his signature moves? **Check out the Neymar Flick tutorial on page 58 of this book and give it a try!**

Club Team:
Santos FC (Brazil)

International Team:
Brazil

10

Club Shirt Number

Previous Clubs

- Santos FC (Brazil)
- FC Barcelona (Spain)
- Paris Saint Germain (France)
- Al Hilal (Saudi Arabia)

Player Award Highlights

- 2 x South American Footballer of the Year (2011, '12)
- FIFA World Cup Dream Team (2014)
- La Liga Best World Player (2014-15)

Team Award Highlights

- UEFA Champions League (2014-15)
- FIFA Club World Cup 2015
- 2 x La Liga (2014-15, '15-'16)
- 5 x Ligue 1: 2017-18, '18-'19, '19-'20, '21-'22, '22-'23)

Career Stats

- Career Appearances: 731
- Career Goals: 442
- Career Assists: 286

NEYMAR

POSITION:
FORWARD

FUN FACT:
Neymar loves funk and rap music. He's perfor[med]
with Brazilian music artists and has shown off [his]
dance moves in various videos.

NEYMAR FLICK

1.
Lock the ball between your feet.

2.
Spring upward, lifting your feet sideways while keeping the ball locked between them.

3.
As you reach the peak of your jump, use the inside of your back foot to flick the ball up and over your opponent's head. While they're confused looking up, sprint around them to collect the ball on the other side.

DIFFICULTY RATING
★ ★ ★ ★ ★

Follow the **three simple steps** for each trick and see if you can master the skills of your favorite players!

1.
Charge directly at the defender with speed.

2.
Just as you reach them, plant your front foot forward as if continuing straight, then use the inside of other foot to chop the ball sharply behind your standing leg.

3.
This sends the ball cutting behind your planted leg, in the opposite direction from where the defender thought you were going, allowing you to accelerate into your new direction for a clean getaway!

DIFFICULTY RATING
★★☆☆☆

SKILLS TUTORIAL

PANENKA PENALTY

1.
Place the ball on the penalty spot and back up for your run-up. Sprint towards the ball as if you are going to kick it with full power.

2.
Instead of smashing it, gently use the top of your foot to dip under the middle of the ball with a soft, controlled touch.

3.
The ball will float lazily up the middle as the goalkeeper dives desperately to either side!

DIFFICULTY RATING
★ ★ ☆ ☆ ☆

This technique is named after **Antonín Panenka**, who used it in the 1976 UEFA European Championship final.

Learning new skills takes **time and patience**. Even the very best soccer stars have to practice! So if you don't succeed the first time, **don't give up**—keep trying!

1.
Using the outside of your foot, push the ball to one side as if you're heading in that direction, but be careful not to push it too far!

2.
Use the inside of the same foot to suddenly catch the ball and move it in the opposite direction, in one fluid movement.

3.
This creates a snapping rubber-band effect that leaves defenders lunging in the wrong direction! They'll think you're going one way, but suddenly you're speeding off in the completely opposite direction.

The elastico, also known as the flip-flap, was a skill often used by **Ronaldinho**.

DIFFICULTY RATING
★★★★☆

DEFENDERS

KEEPERS

VAN DIJK
(Netherlands)
Virgil van Dijk captains both his club and international team. He's played in the 2022 UEFA Euro and FIFA World Cup.

RUDIGER
(Germany)
Antonio Rüdiger earned honors in multiple FIFA and UEFA competitions and was a Best FIFA Men's player (2024).

RÚBIN DIAS
(Portugal)
Rúben Dias helped Manchester win a continental treble, and UEFA Champions League Defender of the '21 season.

GIRMA
(USA)
Naomi Girma won a gold Olympic medal ('24) and was U.S. Soccer Female Player of the Year (2023).

CARVAJAL
(Spain)
Daniel Carvajal Ramos played in the FIFA World Cup (2018, '22) and helped Spain win the UEFA European Championship ('24).

EDERSON
(Brazil)
Ederson Santana de Moraes won the Golden Glove three times in a row: 2019-20 to '21-'22.

ÁLISSON
(Brazil)
Álisson Becker has played in the FIFA World Cup (2018, 22) and won Best FIFA Goalkeeper in 2019.

COURTOIS
(Belgium)
Thibaut Courtois became the youngest senior international goalkeeper at 19 and won a 2018 Golden Glove.

NAEHER
(USA)
Alyssa Naeher's team won the '19 FIFA World Cup, plus a gold and bronze medal in the '24 and '20 Olympics.

MARTÍNEZ
(Argentina)
Emiliano 'Dibu' Martínez and his team won the 2022 FIFA World Cup, and he's won three Golden Gloves, too.

LEGENDS

FUTURE STARS

RAPINOE
(USA)
Megan Rapinoe won the Ballon d'Or Féminin (2019), gold at the 2012 Olympics, and FIFA World Cup (2015, '19).

PELÉ
(Brazil)
Pelé scored more than 1200 goals during his career, and was voted "Athlete of the Century" by the Olympic Committee.

MARADONA
(Argentina)
Diego Armando Maradona Franco won FIFA Player of the 20th Century, and was an important soccer player and manager.

RONALDO (R9)
(Brazil)
Ronaldo Luís Nazário de Lima was FIFA World Player of the Year thrice ('96-'98) and won two Ballon d'Or awards ('97, '02).

RONALDINHO
(Brazil)
Ronaldinho Gaúcho has won many major awards, including a FIFA World Cup ('22), Ballon d'Or ('05), and FIFA World Player of the Year ('04-'05).

HAALAND
(Norway)
Erling Haaland won Golden Boy in 2020, and progressed to most goals in a Premier League Season ('22-'23).

GAVI
(Spain)
Pablo Martín Páez Gavira (a.k.a. 'Gavi') won Golden Boy ('22) and the Kopa Trophy ('22) for best player under 21.

ENDRICK
(Brazil)
Endrick Felipe Moreira de Sousa made a strong impression early in his career, playing for Real Madrid when he turned 18.

GÜLER
(Turkey)
Arda Güler plays midfielder and right winger and joined Real Madrid at 18. He's already showing strong offensive abilities.

RODMAN
(USA)
Trinity Rain Moyer-Rodman has scored nearly 30 NWSL goals in her first four seasons.

NOTES